Biblical Child Discipline Made Plain

Valuable Guidelines for Today's Families

by
Clarence and Susan Montgomery

Copyright © 2018-2021 Clarence Montgomery
All rights reserved

All correspondence can be directed to:
TheMontgomeryLine@gmail.com

ISBN-10: 0-69205-958-X
ISBN-13: 978-0-69205-958-6

Printed in USA

DEDICATION

We humbly dedicate this book to the One who deserves more credit than we could ever give Him, the Lord Jesus Christ. Without a doubt, it is true to say that this book literally would not have been possible without Him. We are honored that He has entrusted us with such a high privilege of participating in the training of the next generation. To God be the glory! Great things He hath done!

ACKNOWLEDGMENTS

Those who have heavily invested into our lives are many, and we will be forever indebted to them. Our seven children have been a tremendous inspiration to us, and we are honored to be their parents and cheerleaders. Our local church, Countryside Baptist Church of Guyton, Georgia, has been a tremendous source of both opportunity and encouragement as we sought to raise children who honor the Lord.

Our gratitude goes to Craig Howard (our son-in-law with Magnifi Media), the graphic designer who created this book's outstanding cover. We're also grateful to Greg Perry, Publisher at Servus Publishing, for making the book available for distribution to others.

CONTENTS

	Introduction	i
Chapter 1	What is Biblical Child Discipline?	3
Chapter 2	The Solid Foundation	5
Chapter 3	Why Use Discipline	11
Chapter 4	Who to Discipline	17
Chapter 5	When to Discipline	29
Chapter 6	What to Use to Discipline	37
Chapter 7	Where to Discipline	49
Chapter 8	How to Discipline	55
	Closing Thoughts	65

INTRODUCTION

My dear parent, disciplining your child can be a daunting task at times. While child discipline is not always an easy task, the path to dealing with it can be made plain. It is not for cowards, but it is for the courageous parents who want something better for their child. As parents, we have seen firsthand the results of these principles in practice. We can only say... they work.

DON'T LET THE CONFUSING VOICES OF THE MEDIA, SOCIETY, AND EVEN YOUR OWN FAILURES, DISTRACT YOU FROM THIS ALL-IMPORTANT DUTY.

My wife Susan and I have been honored to have seven children... three boys and four girls. They were born over a span of twenty-four years. Also, we have been blessed with seven grandchildren with, no doubt, plenty more to come.

Through God's help and wisdom, and through first-hand

experience, we feel we have some proven insights to share for child discipline. While none of our seven children are perfect (*surprise!* ... and neither are we as parents), we have, without a doubt, found the Bible, God's Word, to be our foundation for child rearing. You have everything to gain and nothing to lose by disciplining the proven way!

The result is a group of children who rise up and call you blessed. Children who honor their Creator and their parents. The intent of this book is to put our arms around you and let you know that you absolutely can do it.

Don't let the confusing voices of the media, society, and even your own failures, distract you from this all-important duty. While no home is perfect, it is our passion that the sweetness of tranquility and contentment be experienced in your home.

CHAPTER 1

WHAT IS BIBLICAL CHILD DISCIPLINE?

So, what do we mean by Biblical child discipline? The following illustration may help to explain.

I (Susan) absolutely love working outdoors with potted flowers and plants. It is a healthy diversion for me, and I often lose all track of time. Flowers add such beauty to the house and yard. My goal is to place those flowers and plants in the right environment (sunshine, water, fertilizer, etc.) so that they will thrive.

Early in January, 2018, Southeast Georgia (our home) experienced an extremely rare snowfall. Not having a greenhouse to protect my plants, I did my best to shield my "babies" from the wintery onslaught. They were placed on my patio close to the outside wall of our house and covered with blankets and sheets.

The temperatures at night stayed below freezing for a week. Upon removing the hopefully-protective covers, I was saddened to see a limp, frost-bit mess. Needless to say, those plants *were not* in an environment to help them thrive.

Child discipline is much the same as caring for plants. In fact, the Bible even refers to children as plants.

> *"Thy children like olive plants round about thy table"* (Psalm 128:3).

> *"That our sons may be as plants grown up in their youth"* (Psalm 144:12).

So, how can we, as parents, place our children in the right environment so that they will thrive? That's where child discipline comes in.

A good definition of Biblical child discipline is as follows:

> *Biblical child discipline is the training of children to obey* **immediately, cheerfully,** *and* **completely** *in response to God-appointed authority.*

Three key words… immediately, cheerfully, and completely!

1. *Immediately*: A delayed response from your child ("I'll do it later!") is not true obedience.

2. *Cheerfully*: A complaining, grumpy response ("I hate taking out the trash!") is not true obedience.

3. *Completely*: A sloppy, halfhearted-job response ("I can't help it if there's food still stuck on the dish! At least I washed it!") is not true obedience.

> **Note:** *Discipline is not just correcting children when they do wrong; it includes teaching them how to do right.*

So, with that definition of Biblical child discipline, let's look further into answering some questions about how to help our "plants" thrive.

CHAPTER 2

THE SOLID FOUNDATION

The Leaning Tower of Pisa, a freestanding bell tower, is a famous tourist attraction in Italy. Why is this renowned tower leaning? Only five years after beginning construction in August 1173, the tower began to lean once construction on the second floor began. The soft sand beneath it was the cause. The foundation was not stable.

On the brink of collapse, the tower was saved by a reconstruction project that ended in 2001. A prime example of the importance of a solid foundation!

HAVING A PERSONAL RELATIONSHIP WITH JESUS CHRIST IS THE FIRST STEP TO HAVING A SOLID FOUNDATION. JESUS CHRIST IS THE FOUNDATION.

Your home is no different. The foundation must be level and

sturdy.

> *"For other foundation can no man lay than that is laid, which is Christ Jesus"* (1 Corinthians 3:11).

Having a personal relationship with Jesus Christ is the first step to having a solid foundation. Jesus Christ is the foundation.

We (Susan and I) both made our decisions to have a personal relationship with Christ. I was 16 years old, and Susan was 10 years old when our decisions were made.

Even though Jesus died for the sins of the human race, God did not make us as robots. He longs for us to choose Him.

How can a person have a personal relationship with Jesus Christ?

To make it simple, think of *ABC*.

A - *ADMIT* that you are a sinner and in need of God's forgiveness.

> *"All have sinned and come short of the glory of God"* (Romans 3:23).

When you compare yourself with other people, you might not seem too bad. But when you compare yourself with God, you fall very short.

B - *"BELIEVE* *on the Lord Jesus Christ and thou shalt be saved"* (Acts 16:31).

> Jesus shed His blood to pay for your sin. You can be forgiven, because Jesus died on the cross for you and rose again.

C - *CALL* on Jesus to save you.

> *"For whosoever shall **call** on the name of the Lord shall be saved"* (Romans 10:13).

Once you realize that you are a sinner and that you need God's salvation, it is a matter of you calling on Him to save you. Pray a prayer something like this and mean it with all your heart.

"Dear God, I know that I am sinner. I can do nothing by myself to be right with God. You died for me on the cross. Please forgive me of my sins. Jesus, I invite You into my life to be my Savior. I give my life to You. Thank You for dying for me. Amen."

Without Jesus Christ as our foundation, this book would never have been written because He is the One that made our home successful. And Jesus can do the same for your home!

PRAY FOR YOUR CHILDREN

It has been presented that Christ is the solid foundation; therefore, make it a habit, as parents, to pray for your children. Pray that they would come to have a personal relationship with Christ at an early age. Even show them yourself how to know Christ. What an honor!

Actually, it has been said that it is easier to raise a child that has been born *twice* (physically and spiritually) than it is to raise a child born only *once* (physically). Why? Because a child that knows Christ as his/her Savior has the Holy Spirit living inside to help them make the right choices.

Just as a newborn baby grows physically, a newborn Christian grows spiritually. When Christ comes into a life, He makes a change. *"Therefore, if any man be in Christ, he is a new creature: old things are passed away; behold, all things are become new"* (2 Corinthians 5:17).

Pray for your child's future spouse and their future career. Pray that they will have a heart for God. And… it is always good that your children hear you pray for them.

Lamentations 2:19 well depicts the proper heart-cry of a parent to the Lord for our children. *"Pour out thine heart like water before the face of the Lord: lift up thy hands toward Him for the life of thy young children."*

As a family, get involved in a good Bible-teaching church. Don't just send your children to church... take them yourself.

MEET THE FAMILY

Interspersed throughout this book are personal notes to us from our children. We never asked our children to write these notes for the purpose of including them in this book.

These priceless treasures were saved over the years because the written words meant the world to us as parents.

These meaningful notes from our children are not included in this book to praise ourselves as parents. We are fully aware that without God being our foundation, these notes would have never been written to us in the first place. *"Except the Lord build the house, they labor in vain that build it"* (Psalm 127:1).

On the contrary, these personal notes have become a part of this book in order to encourage readers that it is absolutely possible to raise respectful, God-honoring children.

CHAPTER TAKEAWAY

A solid foundation is vital, and Jesus Christ is that foundation. May we never forget the lesson of the Leaning Tower of Pisa!

Nathan's text to Clarence. No special occasion – just an impromptu text that meant the world to us appears next (July, 2012).

> **"Dad, you and Mom make me proud to be called a Montgomery. The way you have lived your lives and trained your kids has established a legacy that will be felt for generations. Keep being strong."**

CHAPTER 3

WHY USE DISCIPLINE

Attending a military new-recruit graduation from boot camp is a fascinating experience. Young men and women (who just a few weeks before did not even know each other) now march in unison to the cadence call of their superior.

What caused this remarkable transformation in these future defenders our country? Structure and discipline!

Once unfit bodies are now muscular and toned. The once unkempt hair is now neatly groomed. Where wrinkled clothes used to be the norm, now uniforms are neatly pressed.

These fine recruits were not allowed to stay up all hours of the night eating junk food or playing video games. Respect for those in authority was instilled into them.

How were these goals accomplished? Through discipline!

Of course, a home is not a military boot camp, but the principle is the same. Why discipline? When you know why you are doing something, you are motivated to follow through.

So let's find out why discipline is so important. You might ask... is it worth all the effort? You will find out it absolutely is worth every amount of effort because discipline is the back bone of life itself.

THE DESIRED RESULTS OF DISCIPLINE

Why discipline? Though there may be numerous desired results for disciplining our children, we will focus on six.

IF YOU WANT TO SEE YOUR HOME MORE ORDERLY, YOU MUST DISCIPLINE. ORDER BRINGS A CALMNESS THAT WILL DRASTICALLY REDUCE THE STRESS FACTOR.

---

1. To Maintain Order and Structure

Without order and structure, which discipline provides, life would not even be able to function. That is the way the intelligent Engineer, God, designed the universe.

God is a God of order and detail, not chaos. Each day we know what to expect when God causes the sun to rise and set. What if the sunrise was very unpredictable and happened at random times of the day... maybe 7 AM today and 3 PM tomorrow?

Each day we know that we will have a 24-hour timeframe because of the earth's rotation. Every year we know that there will be the variety of the four seasons... spring, summer, fall, and winter.

So, God is the Author of order and detail, not chaos. If you want to see your home more orderly, you must discipline. Order brings a calmness that will drastically reduce the stress factor.

2. To Teach Self-denial

The heart of discipline is the denial of self-interest. The most miserable children (and adults) are those who have not been trained to deny themselves. They think of themselves as #1.

One way self-denial is taught is by having your children do things they do not necessarily enjoy (like family chore duties). As members of the family, everyone needs to contribute.

Self-denial is something that is not promoted by most forms of the media. In fact, the media's propaganda is just the opposite. Often such ideas as the following are promoted...

"You deserve a break today."

"If it feels good, do it."

The spirit of entitlement, which is basically a "you-owe-me" attitude, is devastating to an individual, a home, and a country.

3. To Produce Positive Results

No new parent starts out with the intention of raising negative, rebellious children. Sadly, the finished product ends up that way because something is neglected. That something is loving, yet firm, discipline.

Think of the pet world. An undisciplined dog will jump all over your guests, lick their hands, and soil their clothes with dirty paws. It will step on their shoes.

In general, he is obnoxious. When the dog is out of control, he is an aggravation to you and your guests. It does not have to be that way.

By not disciplining and denying the dog his bad habits, you have encouraged or trained that type of misbehavior. On the other hand, a disciplined dog is a joy to be around and is even awarded a blue ribbon at a dog show.

Now, of course, children are not dogs... but the analogy holds true. There is no glory in having a disobedient child when you can have an obedient one.

4. To Shape the Will of the Child

To shape the will of the child without breaking the child's spirit is the goal of proper child discipline. We want to shape the will so that the child will have a heart for God.

The goal is never to break the spirit by saying harsh, unkind, demeaning remarks to your child in hopes of getting them to do right.

5. To Promote Godly Character

Godly character is the heart of a meaningful life. It takes character on the parent's part to teach character to children. As mentioned earlier, discipline is not just correcting children when they do wrong, but also teaching them how to do right.

6. To Teach Respect for Authority

Mark it down... children most likely will not respect God's authority if they do not first respect your authority as a parent. You are God's representative in your home.

Parents who refuse to discipline are crippling their children spiritually and psychologically. You can make it easy for your child to submit to God by laying the all-important groundwork of discipline.

Having looked at the desired results of proper discipline, let's consider some commonsense reasons to discipline.

COMMONSENSE REASONS TO DISCIPLINE

1. God says to discipline.

After all, God is the Designer of life, and He knows how life is to be lived. Ephesians 6:4 specifically tells fathers to *"bring them (children) up in the nurture and admonition of the Lord."*

Even the Lord Himself loves His children so much that He corrects them. *"For whom the Lord loveth he correcteth; even as a father the son in whom he delighteth"* (Proverbs 3:12).

"As many as I love, I rebuke and chasten (discipline)," says the Lord (Revelation 3:19).

If for no other reason, God's command to discipline should be reason enough. Obedience is what will please God.

2. The child's future hinges on discipline.

The undisciplined child will never know promotions, advancements, and honors that a disciplined child will know. The undisciplined child will never have the security he longs for. Discipline provides security, which is absolutely essential for stable, independent living.

The eternal destiny of the child is often determined by discipline or the lack of it. *"Thou shalt beat him with the rod (referring to proper spanking) and shalt deliver his soul from hell"* (Proverbs 23:14). When children are trained properly, it helps save the child from a life of destruction.

Lack of discipline impairs a child's usefulness. Care enough about your child that you make an issue over misbehavior. A child who has not learned to accept responsibility will greatly limit his usefulness to his future family and community.

3. The value of the child should motivate us to discipline.

The worth of the child to God demands that we make them a priority. They are our inheritance from God. *"Lo, children are an heritage of the Lord: and the fruit of the womb is His reward"* (Psalm 126:3).

We must protect His heritage. God would have never given parents that precious "heritage" (children) without also giving us instructions on how to care for that heritage.

Tell me how you discipline your child, and I'll tell you how much you value your child. It is not an issue of putting controls on your child, but rather an issue of caring enough to protect them with Biblical, practical, proven guidelines.

With so many reasons to discipline, please do not deprive your child of what they need so desperately... loving, yet firm, discipline.

CHAPTER TAKEAWAY

Since children are a heritage from God, parents are instructed by God to love and discipline that precious heritage.

Dale's note to Clarence written in front of a gift book when Clarence was the best man in Dale's wedding appears next (August, 2007).

> "Throughout the past 22 years of my life, you have been my hero. You have spent time with me, encouraged me, disciplined me, and instructed me in all areas of life and godliness. You have walked in a manner that is worth mimicking. I am especially thankful for the way you loved Mama..."

CHAPTER 4

WHO TO DISCIPLINE

Charles and Sheila were having a rather heated discussion about the family finances. Their words were becoming very unkind, and their voice levels were rising. Soon they were accusing and yelling at each other.

In the background, Charles and Sheila were vaguely aware of their two sons bickering over who was playing with a toy first. The sons began to scream at each other, and soon fists began to fly.

In this all-too-common family scenario, who needs to be disciplined?

The answer to... *both* the parents *and* the children need to be disciplined.

"Train up a child in the way he should go" (Proverbs 22:6).

"Correct thy son, and he shall give thee rest; yea, he shall give delight unto thy soul" (Prov. 29:17).

Someone (the parent) has to train and correct; and someone (the child) has to be trained and corrected. To answer to the "who" question is… both your child and you, the parent, must be disciplined.

But it starts with you, the parent!

Parent, you must be a living commercial of what you want your child to become. Children will mirror what they see and hear. Be sure you give them a quality image to mirror. If you want a great image reflected in your children, they must first see that image in you. As the saying goes, the apple doesn't fall far from the tree.

"Practice what you preach" is not a trite statement.

A somewhat humorous story amply illustrates how important it is for us as parents to realize that our children are watching us.

A son went on a car ride with his dad. When they returned home, the mother asked the son, "Well, son, how was your ride with Dad?" The son replied, "Well, we passed two idiots, five morons, seven dumbbells, nine weird-dos, and four knot-heads!"

Oops! More is caught than taught. Let your lifestyle support what you say.

Be realistic. If your child grows up to be like you, would you be pleased? Or more importantly, would God be pleased?

IMPERFECT PARENTS

Sadly, in these recent days, it has been common for some older teens and young adults to reject the Biblical values of their upbringing when they leave home. Why?

While everyone has their own free will to choose the path they will take in life, sadly, too often young adults forsake Biblical values because they have not seen those values consistently modeled at home.

Of course, Christian parents are not perfect, and they will make mistakes. It is so important for children to see their parent model humility when the parent has failed.

The key is... when we do fail as parents, we should apologize to our children. For example... be quick to say things like the following:

"I'm sorry for yelling at you. I should have had my emotions more under control. Will you please forgive me?"

"I'm sorry for being a bad example to you when I____. I want to do better. Will you please forgive me?"

When children observe their parents asking for forgiveness, they see a model that teaches them how to ask for forgiveness when needed.

Perhaps we parents tell our children not to yell and fight with their siblings. But do we, as parents, speak harshly and abrasively with our spouse? What kind of model is that?

It has been said that the greatest gift you can give a child is a mom and dad who love each other.

> **"CHILDREN WILL MIRROR WHAT THEY SEE AND HEAR. BE SURE YOU GIVE THEM A QUALITY IMAGE TO MIRROR."**

While no parent is perfect, we should strive to live before our children so that they will want the same relationship with Christ that we have. They should see a joy and a genuineness about us. We should not act one way at home and another way in public.

While it is true that each grown child has to make a choice for the path they take in life, do all that you can as a parent to remove from them the excuse to use you as a reason for choosing the wrong path.

Probably every parent would say, if they could do it over again, they would do some things differently. We feel the same way about some of our choices. No parent is perfect. It is important that when we do fail as parents, we should be quick to make it right with our children.

BUILD A RELATIONSHIP

It's extremely important to build a close relationship with your children. Start young. Play with your children. Find out what they enjoy. Laugh together. Eat meals together. Rules without a relationship can lead more to rebellion. Don't be on the go so much that you do not slow down enough to simply enjoy each other.

Make memories. It doesn't even have to cost a lot of money to make memories. For instance, some of the most enjoyable times we had with our kids were playing "Kick the Can" in the yard at night or a game that our kids named "Baseball Inside."

For years and years, I (Susan) have carried around a small paper clipping in the back of my Bible to remind me to enjoy my children. It reads, "So where do we begin loving our children? With the routine of today – by making time for them! We can swing, walk, talk, listen, play, and work with the children God has given us. We are not wasting time. We are accomplishing our God-given tasks as mothers (and fathers) – loving our children" (Rita Carver).

Sadly, too often in this fast-paced society (especially in America), it is easy for parents to be so consumed with pursuing careers that the ones that suffer the most are the children. In this scenario, a parents' best waking hours of the day are focused on the career, and the children get the leftovers of the parents' time and energy. How can we effectively influence our children for good if we are not routinely even with them during their best waking hours of the day?

While it is the parents' responsibility to provide for their family, there must be a balance.

When coming to the end of life, people usually do not say, "Oh,

I wish I had spent more time at my job." But rather, "I wish I had spent more time with my family."

RESPONSIBILITY

We live in a day when it seems no one wants to assume responsibility. However, with the privilege of parenting also comes the responsibility of discipline. As parents, it is time we take a long, hard look at ourselves. We cannot blame our children for inappropriate behavior when they only mimic what they have seen in us.

Though it may happen, never expect the character of the child to rise above the character of the leader... the parent. Be honest and realistic in your expectations.

You are the molder of the life placed into your hands... an awesome privilege and responsibility. Your first plan of action should be to discipline yourself as a parent. Sooner or later you must face the music. Believe me, it is better sooner than later.

Once you have accepted the responsibility, you need the second ingredient of resolution.

RESOLUTION

It is as simple as this... you must change if your child is to change. Please be committed enough to yourself and your child to make some personal course corrections where needed.

You must choose to make corrective action. Nothing is going to change if you, as a parent, do not change. To keep on doing what you're doing and expect different results is faulty reasoning.

Listen... the problem is not with the riots in the streets, it is with the babies in the cribs. Or better said, the problem is with the parents who are training these impressionable babies in the cribs.

Now that you have the whole-hearted resolution to discipline, let's find out what resources are available.

RESOURCES

The good news is that you are well-equipped with everything you need to help your child.

Never, never forget... no other person can do the job of disciplining your child like you can. No daycare center, no neighbor, no grandparent, or no friend will ever be able to do the job as well as you, the parent, can do it.

While there are some situations that require someone else to step in and help (as in the case of single parents), you are uniquely equipped to get the job done. A special unique bond exists between you and your child.

Churches, schools, and clubs may assist; but they are no substitute for you. So what are the resources (tools) that can make a perceptive parent discipline in the right way?

Simply stated, the tools are as follows:

1. THE MANUAL, THE BIBLE

At your disposal is the "Owner's Manual" for disciplining your child. You do not have to guess about it... just follow it. To overlook this resource, you do so to your own peril. It has never failed. Don't waste your time trying to reinvent the wheel.

2. LOVE

Believe it or not, it is God that gives you a love for your child, regardless if your child has been adopted or has been given to you by natural birth. That love supersedes any challenge that your child might have... be it mentally, physically, emotionally, spiritually, or otherwise.

In fact, many times those obstacles cause that love to rise to the occasion and reveal itself in exceptional ways. Without this God-given resource of love, discipline would be nothing more than a task to get done.

Love gives the motivation to discipline. What an awesome resource you have available to you. Remember, love is based on commitment, not feelings. There will be days when you don't feel like doing what you should do. Commitment will get you through those kinds of days.

3. ABILITY

God told Adam and Eve in the Garden of Eden to *"be fruitful and multiply"* (Genesis 1:22). He would not have instructed the first man and woman to have children without giving them the resources for the role of parenting.

"Children are an heritage (inheritance) of the Lord," (Psalm 127:3). Just know that God uses all of your experiences... good or bad... to give you the exact ability to train your child. This understanding will give you the confidence that *you* are the one meant for the job of training your child.

4. POWER

To have the manual (Bible), love, and ability, and yet lack the power, the job will not be done correctly. For the committed parent who has a personal relationship with God, this power is accessible through the Holy Spirit.

The challenge of disciplining can be overwhelming at times. Don't try to do this alone. It's a recipe for frustration if you do.

"But you shall receive power after that the Holy Ghost is come up on you" (Acts 1:8). For the Christian parent, the Holy Spirit Who lives inside can help in our weakness.

The Holy Spirit will come along side to help produce the fruit of the Spirit, which is *"love, joy, peace, long-suffering (patience), gentleness, goodness, faith, meekness, and temperance (self-control)"* (Galatians 5:22-23).

5. MENTORS

Another tool to help with parenting is mentors. Look around for a family that you admire... one whose children seem to be well disciplined. Get to know that family. Watch them and their parenting techniques.

Maybe you could be that mentor for a young family. Invite them to your home. Take an interest in their children. Never underestimate the influence you may have on other families by allowing them to watch your life.

To sum it up...the wonderful thing is -- you do not have to go out and purchase the tools to do the job of parenting. You already have everything you need.

Keep in mind... we can only discipline well if we ourselves are well disciplined. So how can we know if we are disciplined parents? Glad you asked.

TEST YOURSELF IN 3 BASIC AREAS

1. TIME

Everyone has the same amount of time each day. President or parent... it makes no difference. God has given us exactly enough time to do what we are supposed to do each day.

If we are not getting some things done that should be done, then either we need to cut out something or make better use of the time we have.

Do you spend excessive amounts of time on social media or on watching TV? Don't squander your time. Let your children see you value your time by making wise choices with it.

Speaking of TV watching habits, do you set an example by watching quality programs that promote righteous values? If you watch TV shows or movies that show extra-marital affairs, do not be surprised if your children practice sex outside of marriage.

Manage your time wisely. Learn the difference between what is important and what is urgent. By the way, what is urgent is not always important! Write out what is important to you and your family.

You will be amazed at how you will use your time on things that are important (if they are written out) instead of on trivial things.

2. MONEY

The use or misuse of money will send a strong message to your children. Don't think for a moment they don't notice how you spend your money. Use it wisely. Let money be your servant, not your master. Money is a wonderful servant, but a terrible master.

Proper money management will eliminate a huge stress factor in your home. To be disciplined in every area, but not in the financial area, will leave a gaping hole in your credibility.

Here are some thought-provoking questions for parents: Do you live on a budget?

Are you an impulsive buyer? Are you in debt?

Money management is an area where we, as parents, must be disciplined and set the right example for our children.

3. LIFESTYLE

How disciplined are you with the vehicle (your body) that will carry you around for your entire life? If we would treat our bodies like a Mercedes when we are young, we wouldn't have to drive around in a beat-up Volkswagen when we are old.

Your lifestyle plays a huge, visible part of how your kids accept or reject discipline.

Consider these three practical tips in living a disciplined lifestyle:

- EAT WELL

Don't swallow the lie about eating only what tastes or looks good. You can't fool your kids on this issue. Let them see you are serious about eating right. The more natural the food is, the better.

If you expect to discipline well, you must eat well.

Are you overweight? Do you exercise self-control in your diet?

Avoid destructive habits such as smoking and drinking alcoholic beverages. They are counterproductive.

Your physical appearance is a constant, visible reminder whether you are disciplined or not disciplined. You are a walking billboard before your kids. What do they see?

There is a direct correlation between your eating habits and other areas of your life. Discipline crosses over into other areas of one's life. Put bluntly, if you can't lead in the visuals, your words and instruction to your children will be seriously diluted.

- EXERCISE OFTEN AND KEEP FIT

You must make it a priority to keep your body in shape. If we cannot be disciplined with our own body, how can we expect our children to be disciplined with theirs?

Susan and I have resolved to keep ourselves fit for each other. We have to work at it, but it is well worth the effort. A minimal amount of exercise and proper eating go a long way.

These three major testing grounds – time, money, and lifestyle – make such a huge difference in your discipline quest. Yes, there are other areas, but if you are disciplined in these areas, you definitely have a head-start.

If an engineer that designed a skyscraper was inaccurate in three major areas, the building with soon collapse.

You cannot afford to be "off" in these major areas of life. Remember, a lack of discipline in one area of life carries over into other areas of life.

QUESTION: In these three categories of *time*, *money*, and *lifestyle*, how would your children rate you on a scale of 1 to 10? If they would give you a low rating, then changes on your part are definitely in order.

It isn't fair to expect your children to turn out differently than what was role-modeled before them for years.

Have the character to make changes in yourself. Then…when those issues arise in your child's life, your life and words will carry weight. Your effectiveness will be greatly enhanced. That son or daughter will have a healthy sense of respect and honor for you.

CHAPTER TAKEAWAY

Parents must be disciplined themselves before they can effectively discipline their children.

Shannon's note to Susan after Shannon had her first baby appears next (July, 2017).

> "Mom, well, what can I say? 'Thank you' doesn't seem to do it justice. While I am so very thankful for the baby shower gifts, I am also overwhelmed by all you have given me as a mom. Thank you for your steady example of leading us kiddos – for being diligent in studying your Bible, making lunches for dad, keeping up with laundry, grocery shopping, and all the billions of other things you do…"

CHAPTER 5

WHEN TO DISCIPLINE

Our adult daughter worked in a local daycare, and her main responsibility was caring for the two-year-olds. The "Terrible Twos."

Often, she would come home extremely frustrated, because the employees were very limited in what they could do to make the children behave. Kids jumping on their cots when they're supposed to be taking a nap. Kids head-butting other children in the group. Kids telling their instructors, *"No!"*

In incidences of blatant disobedience, employees were told to "redirect" the children by trying to get them to forget their misbehavior and become occupied with other activities.

Children are much smarter than we give them credit for! They know when there will be no consequences severe enough to deter their misbehavior.

Proper child discipline should take place *when* the disobedience occurs, and ... child discipline should start way before the *"terrible-two"* years arrive.

Timing is extremely important! To do the right thing at the wrong time will cause a strike out. Just ask a baseball player at bat. He may be swinging at a great pitch, but it doesn't matter if he does it at the wrong time. Nothing runs properly without timing.

For example, the very seasons of the year are perfectly timed. Timing affects the growing seasons. Most types of vegetables are not planted during the winter, because they would not survive the frost. Planting time is in the spring. Timing is crucial.

In addition, a vehicle has to be in perfect timing, or the result is a rough ride. When discipline is in perfect sync with the infraction, the ride is much smoother. The desired effect (results) of discipline is undermined if the discipline is done at the wrong time.

Rule to follow: Discipline for disobedience should follow as soon as possible for maximum effectiveness.

EARLY IS THE WATCHWORD!!!

Early is so important!! Proverbs 13:24 helps us understand this when it says, *"He that spareth his rod hateth his son: but he that loveth him chasteneth (disciplines, corrects) him betimes (early)."*

(Exactly what the "rod" is will be discussed later.)

The old cliché that says, *"Spare the rod and spoil the child"* probably came from this Bible verse.

The key in Proverbs 13:26 is that the parent who truly loves his child will discipline him *early*.

- Early in Life

The earlier you start, the less challenges you will have when the child is older.

To start training a child at 16 years of age can be done, but it would be much easier and effective to start training as a one-year-old. So much grief and hardship can be eliminated by doing it sooner rather than later. And I assure you that you will be richly rewarded by starting today rather than tomorrow!

- Early in Problems

> **"THE EARLIER YOU START TO DISCIPLINE, THE LESS CHALLENGES YOU WILL HAVE WHEN THE CHILD IS OLDER."**

Don't let so much time elapse between the disobedience and the discipline.

For example, if your 10-year-old lied to you at home, deal with it right away. Facts and details of the incident become less and less clear the longer you wait. By waiting, the problem never gets easier or smaller. *"Nip it in the bud"* is a good rule of thumb.

If your child knows you are consistent in dealing with infractions quickly, he will be less likely to engage in borderline behavior. I am referring to behavior that smacks with defiance, such as a smirk or the rolling of the eyes. Both of these gestures should not be tolerated and should be addressed. If left unchecked, it will grow into a more serious issue.

Swift correction always promotes an environment of unity and respect. If you snooze, you lose the opportunity to communicate an important message. The message is that it takes discipline to make it in life.

HOW EARLY SHOULD I START?

How early in my child's life should I start disciplining? It actually starts in the early months of life. Of course, not with spankings, but the teaching process begins in the early months.

What follows are a couple of examples:

SLEEPING HABITS

Teaching your child to sleep in his or her own bed is a form of discipline. If the child is not sick, is fed, and is clean, yet still cries when put down for a nap, it is a good time to let them cry for a while to let them know they will not always be held.

Personally, we never allowed our children to get into the habit of sleeping with us (except for the first few weeks after giving birth during the recovery and adjusting time). A couple of reasons for this early discipline of the sleeping habits comes to mind.

1. Allowing the child to sleep with you will be an extremely hard habit to break when they get older.

2. Allowing your child to habitually sleep with you is a huge deterrent to intimacy with your spouse.

CHURCH NURSERY

Another early discipline might involve leaving your baby in the church nursery. Most mothers naturally want to keep their newborn with them in the services for a few weeks. We did as well.

However, putting the baby in the nursery when one to two months old works best for a couple of reasons:

1. The sweet bundle can be a distraction to others in the service.

2. Waiting until the child is very aware of their surroundings will tend to make it harder for the baby to adjust to the new setting of the nursery. When leaving a child in the nursery, assure them of your love, hand them to the nursery worker, and leave the room. Seeing you there will make it harder for the child to adjust.

So, there are some situations when discipline starts in the early months.

REDIRECTING

When babies first become mobile (crawling and walking), redirecting has its place for training. At first, redirecting involves removing them from an unacceptable activity and lovingly, yet firmly, telling them *no*.

This is a foundational timeframe of teaching what is expected. It is crucial during this redirecting stage that the child be with a loving, firm parent.

Usually, this redirecting process has to be repeated often for them to understand. Consistency is the key. Sometimes a slight pop on the hand or the leg may be necessary in this stage of training.

Discipline is teaching the young child the difference between right and wrong. It involves rewarding good behavior and saying no to bad behavior. The "terrible twos" do not have to be so terrible if these foundational principles of discipline are started in the early months and the first year of the child's life.

The time for a spanking comes when there is direct defiant behavior for an action that the child has been taught to be wrong. (How to give an effective spanking is discussed in the chapter entitled *How to Discipline*.)

Please do not depend on a childcare facility to discipline your child. There is very little that they can do in regard to consequences for misbehavior. When it comes to discipline, it is understandable that parents want to guard their child against the possible risk of child abuse by care givers. But why even put your child in the care of someone that you cannot totally trust to discipline them when they misbehave?

Each new parent has to learn how to parent. A few of the discipline techniques that we used with our first child, we changed with the other children. We have jokingly told our oldest child that he was our "guinea pig." But he survived just fine.

COMMON REASONS TO DISCIPLINE

1. Defiant Behavior

Defiant behavior is when told to do something, the opposite is done.

Defiant behavior always needs to be addressed immediately and early in your child's life.

If children do not learn to immediately respond to their parents in a respectful manner, they will most likely grow up not responding to other authorities and to God in a respectable manner.

2. Whining

Whining may seem like a small thing, but it can be the start of a major problem. *Nip it!* It is a sign of a spirit of ingratitude and entitlement, which is very contagious and destructive.

Often whining reveals the child has *too* much and is taking what he does have for granted. They act as if it is their *right* to have certain things. If you detect this whining spirit, do not allow your child to have more things or privileges until this attitude has changed.

Make sure that you as the parent are not guilty of complaining and whining. If you are guilty, admit it, and ask the children to forgive you of this awful sin of ingratitude. Remember... more is caught than taught! You are the role model.

Set a policy in your home to never allow complaining. Practice having a set time when you focus on being grateful for what you have.

Whining can be easily addressed by setting family policy and restricting privileges if violated. Perhaps have the child sit on the couch for a period of time or take a time out to think about his actions. We live in a self-centered world, so you must continually battle this foe of whining.

3. Sibling Rivalry

Sibling rivalry includes both hitting and arguing. Anywhere there are two or more siblings, there will most likely be conflict at some time or other. It is human nature to want our own way, and it is important to let your kids know what is acceptable in your home and what is not. Also, be sure unity is modeled before them by you and your spouse.

If they persist in arguing, playing apart is probably the short-term solution. Calling ugly names and/or hitting is absolutely unacceptable and should warrant a spanking. To tolerate this kind of behavior is like tolerating just a little poison in your food.

4. Lying

Lying is an action that should never be tolerated. It may seem innocent at first, but like a venomous snake, it will bite at the last. If your children are old enough to understand what the truth is, then they should be expected to tell the truth. If they knowingly tell a lie, a spanking would be in order.

God hates lying. *"Lying lips are abomination to the Lord: but they that deal truly are his delight"* (Proverbs 12:22). Train them to love the truth enough to tell it.

> **Note:** Whenever a child chooses to come to you to tell you that he has disobeyed, be fair and take that into consideration. Praise your child for being honest. However, their confession should not always negate the consequences of the misbehavior.

Do not wait until your child is a teenager to start disciplining. Although better late than never, it is much harder on both parent and child if you wait.

CHAPTER TAKEAWAY

Begin *early* in your child's life with properly-timed, age-appropriate, loving discipline. It will be an asset to both your home and your child. If you haven't started early, these principles applied will still effectively work.

Candace's note to Clarence before her wedding appears next (August, 2016).

> "As it gets closer to the wedding, I just am realizing more and more all you have done and sacrificed on my behalf. I have been invested into so much. I love and adore you and mom, and I don't say it near enough. Apart from marrying Jordan, the thing that I look forward to most on my wedding day is walking down the aisle on the arm of the man I first learned to love and respect with all my heart."

CHAPTER 6

WHAT TO USE TO DISCIPLINE

David, king of Israel, became so involved in his career that he lost control of his home. He was a great king, but a terrible father.

One of his sons, Adonijah, tried to exalt himself to reign as king instead of David. Scripture gives us a strong hint for the cause of Adonijah's rebellion.

"Then Adonijah... exalted himself, saying, I will be king: and he prepared him chariots and horsemen, and fifty men to run before him. And his father (David) had not displeased him at any time in saying, Why hast thou done so?" (1 Kings 1:5-6).

David, as his father, *"had not displeased"* Adonijah at any time. In the Hebrew language, "displeased" means pained. David had never "at any time" pained his son by disciplining him in order to show him the error of his ways.

The right kind of discipline involves pain. In this chapter we will discuss the various types of "pain" that can be used in child discipline.

To do the right thing (discipline), but with the wrong tools makes the situation very unpleasant.

Think about it... if a carpenter used a sledge-hammer instead of a framing hammer to build a house, the job could be done, but it would take a lot longer. Also, the finished product would not be as pretty. It is of utmost importance to use the proper tools.

God understands that we, as parents, have an extremely important job... to love, train, and discipline our children. And He would never have given us this precious heritage of children without giving us some guidelines on what to use to properly care for and train them.

GOD'S SPECIFIC INSTRUCTIONS

Here are some specific instructions about child discipline from God to us as parents.

> *"Train up a child in the way he should go: and when he is old, he will not depart from it"* (Proverbs 22:6).

> *"And, ye fathers, provoke not your children to wrath: but bring them up in the nurture and admonition of the Lord"* (Ephesians 6:4).

> *"Chasten thy son while there is hope, and let not thy soul spare for his crying"* (Proverbs 19:18).

> *"Children, obey your parents in all things: for this is well pleasing unto the Lord. Fathers, provoke not your children to anger, lest they be discouraged"* (Colossians 3:20-21).

THE GOAL

The goal of child discipline is to teach the child to listen to your voice and obey. *To speak once in a normal tone of voice and have them respond immediately, cheerfully, and completely should be your goal.*

Delayed obedience is disobedience. Unhappy obedience is disobedience. Incomplete obedience is disobedience. You see, if we do not require immediate, cheerful, and complete obedience, we are actually training our children to disobey.

"THE DISCOMFORT OF THE DISCIPLINE SHOULD ALWAYS OUTWEIGH THE PLEASURE OF THE DISOBEDIENCE."

An immediate, cheerful, and complete response to your normal tone of voice at the first request is the true definition of obedience. And it is obedience that brings about true joy and satisfaction to both the child and parent.

THE TOOL BOX

Three tools to use in discipline will be covered in this section.

Proverbs 29:15 gives us two of the tools.

"The ROD and REPROOF give wisdom: but a child left to himself brings his mother to shame."

A brief overview of the tools is as follows:

- **Rod:** Instruments such as a switch, a small wooden paddle, or a belt.
- **Reproof:** Speaking the truth in love and caring enough to confront.
- **Ratchet:** Privileges granted or withheld.

A very important rule of thumb is... *the discomfort of the discipline should always outweigh the pleasure of the disobedience.* If it does not, you are actually training the child that it pays to do wrong. Even though the discipline may have been unpleasant, in the child's mind, it may be worth the pleasure of the misbehavior.

Some discipline issues will require a spanking (*rod*), other issues will require talking or explaining (*reproof*), while other issues will necessitate privileges being withdrawn or given (*ratchet*). It takes wisdom from God to know which tool to use at any given time because children have varying personalities.

Please remember... the ultimate goal in any child discipline is to help your child develop a heart for God. The goal is not to prove that you are the boss.

The goal is to have a parent/child relationship that helps to lead the child to know God. Why? If a child does not learn to respectfully and obediently respond to his parent, he most likely will not respectfully and obediently respond to God.

Let's take a closer look at these three tools used in child discipline.

THE ROD (SPANKING)

Even though the rod is being addressed first, that does not mean that it is always the first answer in every discipline challenge. Spanking is not the only form of discipline.

The word "spank" is never used in the Bible. Scripture uses the word "rod."

The main child discipline verses are found in the book of Proverbs.

The following are several discipline verses found in Proverbs:

> *"He that spareth his rod, hateth his son; but he that loveth him, chasteneth him betimes (early)"* (Proverbs 13:24).

> *"Foolishness is bound in the heart of a child, but the rod of correction shall drive it far from him"* (Proverbs 22:15).

> *"Withhold not correction from the child: for if thou beatest him with the rod, he shall not die. Thou shalt beat him with the rod, and shalt deliver his soul from hell"* (Proverbs 23:13-14).

> *"The rod and reproof give wisdom: but a child left to himself, bringeth his mother to shame"* (Proverbs 29:15).

So, we definitely see that the Bible supports spanking.

Spanking is never a very pleasant task, but if done correctly, it can be a time that truly bonds you to your child. Let's be clear... when properly done, spanking your child is one of the greatest forms of love you will ever show for your child.

The "no spank" philosophy sounds good on the surface, but it is inherently evil. God's Word and His way is always right. It always has been, and for us to try to improve upon it is an exercise in futility.

In Proverbs 23:13-14 where it says to *"beat him with a rod,"* child abuse is *not* implied.

The word for "rod" is the Hebrew word "shavet." It indicates a thin stick or switch used to administer a small amount of physical pain without lasting physical injury.

It should never injure or cut. How to properly give a spanking is covered in "How to Discipline" (Chapter 8).

The following two Scripture passages warn parents never to abuse their power and authority to provoke their children.

> *"And, you fathers, provoke not your children to wrath: but bring them up in the nurture and admonition of the Lord"* (Ephesians 6:4).

> *"Fathers, provoke not your children to anger, lest they be discouraged"* (Colossians 3:21).

Spanking should always be done in love... never to vent a parent's frustration!

WHEN SHOULD I SPANK?

Spanking should be used when the child shows defiance to *clear* limits.... never for a parent to vent anger or frustration in the heat of the moment.

What is meant by *clear* limits?

Whenever we discipline our children (whether it is a spanking or not), we need to, first of all, make sure that what we expect is clearly understood by the child.

For instance, when we walk through the living room while the TV is on and tell our kids to pick up the toys, we should not assume that they heard us. The instruction is not clear.

Giving your child clear instructions includes the following:

- Eye-to-eye Contact
- Repeat-after-me Instruction

Make sure eye contact is made with your children when you tell them what you want them to do. And after you tell them, have them repeat after you what you said.

Then, if the child chooses to disobey, you will have the confidence to know that they clearly understood your expectations.

Defiant behavior is the child purposefully doing the opposite of what you told them to do. Spanking is also appropriate for such things as stealing, lying, and being disrespectful.

Spanking is not appropriate for childish irresponsibility... things like accidentally spilling a drink or breaking a plate. Even we as adults accidentally spill a drink and break a dish occasionally.

Now if a child purposefully slams his dish on the floor... that is a different story. That is defiant behavior.

We understand there are those who differ on this issue of spanking. But God's way is always right and best. We have sought to follow His way and have absolutely no regrets.

Yes, it is difficult sometimes to do it God's way; but in the end, you will see that it was actually the easier way. Please don't shortchange your kids by doing just what is convenient for you. Both the parent and the child is best served by disciplining God's way. It should not be a matter of convenience, but rather a matter of obedience to God.

Are you willing to trust what God says or live by your feelings?

REPROOF (YOUR WORDS)

The second tool to use in discipline is reproof. When you use reproof (words) to correct your child, be sure you tell them what they did wrong, tell them the penalty, and then carry out what was promised.

For instance, your conversation with your 10-year-old son might go something like this:

"John, you failed to take out the trash. You know it is important for you to do your part as a member of the family. God wants you to do your job well, cheerfully, and when it's supposed to be done. If we see you have consistently done this job well, we will reward you. If you don't do the job correctly, then you will have to give up something you really enjoy doing. John, the choice is yours. We love you, son, and believe in you."

Reproof should be coupled with creativity and an understanding spirit. For instance, if your child does spill a drink, let the child participate in the cleanup process. You might also say, "Let's put our cup further away from the edge of the table and see if that will help prevent a spill."

Here's another creative tip to use reproof (your words) in getting your child to pick up toys. Use your words to mentally prepare them for the task of picking up toys. You might say, "You have five minutes to play and then playtime is over. We will set a timer for five minutes, and when the timer goes off, you must pick up your toys." Giving them that verbal five-minute warning really helps.

Set a timer for five minutes so that the child can actually hear it go off. Let them associate the timer going off with "times up" for playing, and now is the time to pick up.

Be sure to enforce what you have initiated though. If you don't enforce it, you are actually telling your child that you cannot be trusted to keep your word.

What if they don't pick up after the five-minute timer goes off? Their disobedient response then turns into defiant behavior, because they are not doing what you clearly asked them to do.

The manner in which you use your words carries an awesome amount of weight. *"Life and death are in the power of the tongue"* (Proverbs 18:22).

You can crush the spirit of your son or daughter with the explosive power of your words. On the other hand, appropriate, well-timed words can have enormous power to carry your child throughout the tough times of life.

Our advice is... let your words be few, truthful, kind, and appropriate. The way you say your words is as important as the words themselves.

> **REMINDER!** Always follow through with what you say. Sometimes parents say things like, "I'm going to spank you if you don't stop …."

Actually, what the parent is doing is using that statement as a threat in hopes of getting the child to stop misbehaving. Never say that you will spank, unless you intend to do it. If you don't follow through, you are teaching your child that they cannot trust your words.

In addition to the rod and reproof, there is one other tool that is very effective in child discipline. It is the ratchet.

THE RATCHET

A ratchet is a tool used by a mechanic to repair vehicles. It is used to tighten up or loosen up bolts. Without the use of this critical tool, a mechanic would be greatly handicapped.

Discipline, by its nature, can be seen as negative (tightening up). However, it does have a positive side too (loosening up). If a child demonstrates responsibility, privileges should be added. Positive reinforcement is always a healthy and Biblical method. You are teaching them that God rewards responsible behavior.

For example, if your son loves to play with his skateboard and would sacrifice anything for it, you might use this type of scenario. If he continues to "forget" to take out the trash or clean his room, then the privilege of skateboarding would be withdrawn for a day or two.

When considering the use of the ratchet method of discipline, think… what activities does my child enjoy? What would be a big deal if it were taken from him for a time? Be sure the privileges withdrawn are severe enough to motivate the child to not want to repeat the infraction again.

On the other hand, if the child consistently makes his bed or does some other task, you would want to recognize him for it. Granting him additional time to play a sport or some activity he enjoys would be his reward for being faithful with a particular task. Praise and privileges are effective when the child assumes responsibility.

The following is an example of rewarding your child for good computer-time behavior.

You might say something like this to your child, "Sherry, you know we already agreed that you could use the computer for only one hour each day. And if you went over, you would forfeit going to your friend's house. But we noticed that you have been very responsible not to exceed that time limit. Therefore, if you would like, you can invite a friend to come with us for the weekend trip to the mountains. We're proud of you. You're showing us that you're growing up. Keep up the great work."

Good behavior should be rewarded. Bad behavior should result in privileges withdrawn. That is an important life lesson to learn early.

Tightening up or loosening up the privileges depends on the degree of responsibility. An important life lesson is being taught by using this technique. Don't pass up the teachable moments! Privileges and responsibilities are inseparable.

God will give you the wisdom to "tighten up or loosen up" if you ask Him. Use the ratchet wisely, and your child will be destined to have a meaningful and useful life.

A word to the wise… choose your battlefield wisely. Don't fight discipline battles that you are likely to lose. In other words, determine which areas are worthwhile to address. Making issues over which brand of socks to wear, eating all of your food every time, or what to drink for breakfast are examples of areas over which not to make issue.

Certainly, these areas need to be decided, but there is plenty of room for flexibility. Don't major on the minor areas.

CHAPTER TAKEAWAY

The proper tools for discipline are very important. The ROD, REPROOF, and the RATCHET are all tools of love. Use them wisely. Ask God for wisdom, and He will give it to you (James 1:5).

Brooke's text to Susan, while employed in another state appears next (December, 2015).

> "Mama, remember the note you wrote to me when I was home... it had a verse on it and you told me you were praying for me? This morning I pulled out that note in my Bible. You will never ever realize how much of a blessing it was to me today. The Lord definitely knew I needed to read that verse you wrote me. I love you, Mama! I look up to you so much..."

CHAPTER 7

WHERE TO DISCIPLINE

Have you ever attended a little-league ball game and heard a parent try to correct his/her child from the stands? The child was yelled at for everything done wrong, and other spectators heard it all.

"You should've caught that ball!"

"You need to run faster!"

"I can't believe you struck out!"

The kid probably felt like crawling under the bench in the dugout.

Sadly, over the years in our own children's little-league days, we heard some parents engage in this type of poor behavior. You can't help but feel badly for the struggling player.

Yelling from the stands is not where a parent should teach a child how to play ball. Encouraging words, not demeaning words, should be heard from the stands.

The teaching is best done by spending quality, one-on-one time practicing in the yard with the child.

There is a proper time and place to train and correct, but it is not in front of everyone else.

Likewise, the time and place of child discipline is equally important.

Discipline should start in the home. This is the acid test. If it works at home, it works. If it doesn't work at home, then don't try to export it.

ALWAYS DISCIPLINE IN PRIVATE

Always take the child aside to a private place away from the eyes and ears of others. A bedroom or some similar place would be suitable. By correcting your child in front of peers or family members, you are not only embarrassing the child, but humiliating him.

> "ALWAYS TAKE THE CHILD ASIDE TO A PRIVATE PLACE TO DISCIPLINE AWAY FROM THE EYES AND EARS OF OTHERS."

Do not make a spectacle of your child. Often this is done by adults who are attempting to make themselves look superior in the presence of others. Serious emotional and relational damage can be inflicted on the child if discipline is done publicly.

By dealing with them privately, you are saying that you respect them and that you are not interested in exploiting their errors. You have their best interest at heart by giving them the courtesy of privacy.

If possible, always discipline wherever the infraction occurred.

Take the child aside into the nearest private place possible. The home is the most suitable place, but understandably, not always available.

If the misbehavior is not a major incident, take them aside and talk with them about the inappropriate behavior. But... never let unacceptable actions go unchallenged just because you are not at home. The child will take it as an approval of their misbehavior.

If the issue would require a spanking, then use the nearest location that would be out of the hearing and sight of others. If you are only minutes away from home, it would be best to deal with the child when you get home. If you are on vacation, don't wait several days to deal with it.

TEMPER TANTRUMS IN PUBLIC

Very important.... we have found that the "out-of-home" incidences of misbehavior will be very few if you consistently discipline the child at home. Do yourself a favor, and begin early at home first!

Children may be more apt to think they can get away with misbehavior in public. They may think you are less likely to follow through with your consequences because you will be embarrassed by their demands. On the other hand, they will be more apt to obey knowing there will be consequences.

But what if a child throws a temper tantrum or shows some other defiant behavior in public?

At the grocery store, for instance? Here are some tips.

1. Chose a time to shop when the child is well rested. Even we, as adults, are more tempted to be grumpy when we are tired.

2. Before you ever leave home or before you get out of the vehicle, talk with your child. It's important that the child knows what you expect while in the store.

3. Perhaps promise a small reward at the end of the shopping

spree if the child behaves well. Maybe promise to put their favorite snack in the grocery cart right before you check out. This doesn't have to be a regular occurrence, but an occasional reward is always special.

But what if they still throw a tantrum or are defiant?

1. Don't raise your voice to them in the store. How heartbreaking and unpleasant to hear a parent/child yelling-match in the store.

2. Calmly stroll the grocery cart to a more private place in the store, hopefully where there are no other customers.

3. Calmly talk to the child and remind them of your earlier conversation before you started shopping.

4. If need be, leave the cart, pick up the child (or take him/her by the hand) and walk out the store.

5. If talking to them outside the store doesn't work, go home and administer discipline in the privacy of your home. We personally would spank for this kind of defiant behavior.

The key is to make the discipline hurt worse than the pleasure of the disobedience.

6. Definitely don't reward the child with any of the special snacks that you may have promised earlier if they would have behaved.

If you consistently administer the discipline properly and firmly when an "out-of-home" misbehavior experience occurs, your child will get the message that you mean what you say.

CHAPTER TAKEAWAY

Where should I discipline my child? The answer is (1) in a private place and (2) at the nearest place where the misbehavior happened.

Wherever the place that you perform your loving duty of discipline, be assured it is a holy and sacred place. Your sacrifice of obedience to God will be rewarded beyond your wildest imagination. God has given you all the needed tools to properly discipline your child.

Aaron's birthday wishes to Clarence appears next (December, 2017).

> **"Dad, you have made such a positive impact in my life, and I thank you for that. You have taught me to be a man that honors God and treats others with respect. Thank you for always being there for us. Love you."**

CHAPTER 8

HOW TO DISCIPLINE

When I (Clarence) was a lad of approximately thirteen years of age, my job was to provide bedding for the livestock we had on our farm.

A calamity happened when I was attempting to break the twine on a bale of straw. I was using a hooked knife, not exactly the choice standard operating tool.

As soon as the twine broke (with my leg in the line of fire), I pulled the knife through my pants and my upper thigh. My "reward" for not knowing *how* to properly cut the twine was eighteen stitches. That was a high cost for not knowing how to do it correctly.

Doing the job properly could have easily averted a lot of unnecessary pain.

Similarly, knowing *how* to discipline has huge advantages.

ATTITUDE CHECK

Learning how to discipline starts with developing the proper attitude. Attitude is everything. It is the brick and mortar that builds a God-honoring, meaningful life.

What is your attitude toward your children? Do you view them as a bother or a blessing? Either way, that attitude will shine through in your words and actions.

Some parents might say… "I wish my children were older so that I can get out and be involved in a 'ministry.' Put bluntly, your children *are* your ministry.

Talent or personality is not enough to have a successful, finished product of a disciplined, respectful child. It takes a positive attitude to make positive changes. Your attitude is what you are, and that will overflow into how you act.

Focusing on your child's strengths, not faults, will promote a more positive attitude. All of us (both you and your child) have weak areas on which we need to work. We all make mistakes, but our failures need never be final nor fatal.

"A just (righteous) man falleth seven times and riseth up again" (Proverbs 24:16).

This is a negative world, but we can counter negativism by emphasizing the positive. Kids pick up on your general attitude, and specifically on the way you deal with them. Set the tone by not always focusing on your child's negative traits, and begin emphasizing their positive actions.

A good way to eliminate the negatives is to use the following formula: *For every criticism, give two or three compliments.*

Create a positive spirit in your home! This is a great exercise for a great attitude. A positive attitude sets the environment for more effectively disciplining your child.

DISCIPLINE GUIDELINES

Here are four discipline guidelines... be *clear*, be *swift*, be *fair*, and be *firm*.

"THE DESIRED END IS FOR THE CHILD TO HAVE A HEART FOR GOD."

- BE CLEAR when defining the rules. Don't overlook anything. Spell out what you expect... especially when dealing with the younger children. Here again, you can even have them repeat back to you what you expect.

- BE SWIFT in dealing with discipline. Of course, make sure you get all of the facts, but don't waste a lot of time negotiating. Get to the issue and get on with life. Your child will be the better for it. Don't drag out issues that should be resolved in a timely manner.

- BE FAIR. It is never right to be unkind or inconsiderate just because we, as parents, may be bigger physically. Your credibility will be severely damaged if you are not sincere, kind, and fair. You have the capability to crush their spirits, but don't give in to the temptation.

- BE FIRM in sticking by the "rules of the game." A ball game is much more enjoyable if the umpire enforces the rules with a degree of authority. You open yourself up to all kinds of criticism and frustration if you are not consistent in following the rules.

Once boundaries are in place, have the fortitude to enforce them. Someday your kids will thank you for doing so. No, you are not a dictator, but there must be a leader who leads with a measure of resolve.

In Chapter 4 we talked about the three tools to use for discipline... the *rod*, *reproof*, and the *ratchet*. It surely does take God's wisdom to know when and how to use each of these tools of discipline.

DEFIANT BEHAVIOR

The rod (spanking) is definitely appropriate for defiant disobedience. Defiant disobedience includes such things as:

- Verbal disrespect of parents
- Disrespectful body language (like rolling of the eyes, stamping the foot, temper tantrum)
- Lying
- Stealing
- Purposefully disobeying clearly-defined rules

HOW TO GIVE A SPANKING

Before the Spanking

- Make sure your child understands the clearly-defined rules. When explaining what you expect, make sure there has been (1) the eye-to-eye contact and (2) the "repeat-after-me" process (discussed in an earlier chapter).
- Use wisdom. If ever we, as parents, need wisdom... it is now. Always pray for God's wisdom (silently, if necessary) in dealing with your child.
- Get all the facts... especially when more than one child is involved in the incident.
- Always bring your child aside into a private area. We typically took our children into a bedroom and closed the door. Please never grab them up in frustration and swat them in front of others. Swatting them in front of others is embarrassing for the child. It can cause more damage than good,

because a swat really doesn't hurt enough. *Remember, the discomfort of discipline **must** exceed the pleasure of doing wrong.*

- In a normal tone of voice, assure them that you love them. This is not a time to flaunt your authority.

- Clearly tell them what their offense was and the punishment required.

- Let them know the offense was not *just* against another sibling, parent, friend, etc., but more importantly, against God. What an opportunity to set the stage for God to have their heart! Here is a teachable moment. God is the ultimate authority, and it is to Him that we must give account. The sooner this is learned, the better life will be.

- Tell them that you love them too much to let them get by with doing wrong. Tell them that doing wrong always brings hurt to themselves and others.

During the Spanking

- Only spank on the buttocks... no other part of the body, such as the face or limbs. It is *never*... I repeat *never*... correct to slap on the face, yank on the ears, jerk on the limbs, and so on. This type of action only reveals a parent that is out of control!

- The best position for spanking a younger child (ages 1 to 5) is to have the child bend over the lap of the parent. An older child can lean across the edge of the bed. Parental discretion is certainly in order as to what position is suitable.

- Using an object to administer discipline is more suitable than using your hand. The paddle or belt can inflict enough pain to communicate the message that disobedience hurts and creates pain. Using your hand typically does not inflict enough pain (except for pain in the parent's hand). For the younger children (approximately ages 1 to 7), we used a small wooden paddle. For the older children (ages 8 and older), we used a belt.

- Always speak in a normal tone of voice. Yelling or any type of abnormal behavior should be taboo. Even though it is a very emotional time, determine that you will be calm and under control.

- Spank hard and long enough to break their will. This is often detected in the child's cry, attitude, and demeanor. If you child still has a cocky attitude after you have given a spanking, then you did not spank hard enough or long enough. *The discomfort MUST outweigh the pleasure of the disobedience.*

- **TIP:** *Remember that you are doing the child one of the greatest services by spanking them when the occasion calls for it. You are doing the child a disservice by neglecting to spank when it is needed.*

Some parents may say, "I love my child too much to spank." However, the Bible says that the opposite is true. Proverbs 13:24 tells us, *"He that spareth his rod (fails to spank when needed) hateth his son: but he that loveth him, chasteneth (disciplines) him betimes (early)."* If a parent really loves his child, that parent will be willing to spank him when the occasion calls for it.

After the Spanking

- Very important! If after the child receives a spanking, he immediately repeats the same offense or is defiant, you probably either did not spank hard enough or long enough. As mentioned earlier, the pain must outweigh the pleasure of the disobedience.

- After spanking, assure them again of your love. This is best done by holding or hugging them for a while. Hold them in silence for several minutes if need be. Let them hold or hug you as long as they need to. *Do not rush this time.*

- Pray with your child, saying something like this, "Dear God, help____(child's name) to know that You love him/her very much and that I love him/her too. Thank You that you will help_ (child's name) to do right. Amen."

- Now lead your child in prayer by saying something like this: "_(child's name), let's tell God that you are sorry for __ (whatever offense was)." If the child is quite young, lead them in prayer in short phrases and have them repeat after you saying something like this: *"Dear God, I'm sorry for __. Please forgive me. Help me not to___*(name the offense).

- Tell them that you love them and believe in them before leaving the room.

- Always let them have a few minutes by themselves if they desire. This often gives them time to rethink what happened and to regain their composure.

SOME DISCIPLINE "NEVERS"

- After dealing with your child's disobedience, never bring up their past failures. God does not do that to us. The past is the past. Let your kids know that you will not use the past against them.

- Never interfere with your spouse who is doing the disciplining. Talk through discipline policies beforehand behind closed doors. Disagreeing with your spouse about discipline issues in front of your child sends a mixed message. It tells them, "You don't have to listen to your dad or mom." Telling a child he does not have to listen to either parent can cause them to rebel against that parent. This is especially crucial for wives to be supportive of their husband's leadership role.

- Never ask your child to disrobe while spanking him. To undress in your presence is not necessary. Adequate punishment can be given without having them undress.

- Never say things like, "You can't do anything right" or "You'll never amount to anything." Never call your child names like "Stupid." Never say statements that compares one child with another... "Why can't you be like your brother/sister?" This should not be an occasion to take advantage of them. Let them hear you say words of security and affirmation.

- Never feel sorry for the child that has been disciplined. You are preparing them for life. Don't "baby" them after a spanking by giving them special favors, privileges, etc. Yes, love them, to be sure, but do not cater to their painful experience.

- Never allow the child to play on the emotions of one parent against the other. Both parents should treat the child in the same way.

- Never discipline in a fit of rage. More harm than good is done if this happens. You should never jerk your child up or yell at him/her. This is counterproductive. When you yell, you are showing your child that you are out of control. *"A soft answer turneth away wrath, but a grevious words stir up anger"* (Proverbs 15:1).

OUR HEAVENLY FATHER, OUR MODEL

The Bible tells fathers and mothers in Hebrews 12:5-11 to parent their children the same way that God parents His children.

> *"My son, despise not thou the chastening (disciplining) of the Lord, neither faint when thou art rebuked of him: for whom the Lord loveth he chasteneth, and scourgeth every son whom he receiveth. If ye endure chastening, God dealeth with you as with sons; for what son is he whom the father chasteneth not?"*

No discipline (even in our own lives as God's child) feels good while it is happening, but afterwards (if we respond properly), it yields rich rewards.

What kind of rich rewards does God's discipline yield? It yields godly character, peace, patience, contentment... just to mention a few. This should be the same for our human children.

Children who have learned to take responsibility for their own actions are happier people. *"Happy is the man (person) that findeth wisdom, and the man that getteth understanding"* (Proverbs 3:13).

CHAPTER TAKEAWAY

Though the pain of discipline is not pleasant at the time, the ultimate and most important goal of our child discipline should be to steer the heart of our child toward Jesus and the forgiveness of sin that He offers. *The desired end is for our child to have a heart for God.*

Parents should teach their children to obey so that, at an older age, when God tells the child what to do, they will readily obey Him. If they are not accustomed to obeying you as a parent, they most likely will not obey God.

Hannah's birthday wishes to her dad appears next (December, 2017).

> "I'm glad I have a daddy like you. I enjoy our dates a lot and look forward to them. So happy birthday. Love ya."

CLOSING THOUGHTS

A happy home? Everyone wants it, but not everyone is willing to pay the price to get it. You have everything to gain and nothing to lose by disciplining the proven way.

Every man and woman that has ever accomplished anything noteworthy has learned to be disciplined. In fact, we enjoy the freedoms, liberties, and even the conveniences of life because of those that were disciplined in the past... for example, our incredible military personnel.

Discipline can be a very positive thing. Perhaps the most positive thing you could do for your child is to discipline him. And dear parent, always remember, you do not have to do it alone. God wants to help you more than you may realize.

Happy Parenting!

www.ingramcontent.com/pod-product-compliance
Lightning Source LLC
LaVergne TN
LVHW051158080426
835508LV00021B/2679